WANTED:

COMEDY, ADDICTS

WANTED:

COMEDY, ADDICTS

WANTED:

COMEDY, ADDICTS

WANTED:

COMEDY, ADDICTS

WANTED:

COMEDY, ADDICTS

WANTED:

COMEDY, ADDICTS

WANTED:

COMEDY, ADDICTS

WANTED:

COMEDY, ADDICTS

WANTED:

COMEDY, ADDICTS

WANTED:

Wanted: Comedy, Addicts
© AR Dugan / Cathexis Northwest Press

No part of this book may be reproduced without written permission of the publisher or author, except in reviews and articles.

First Printing: 2021

Paperback ISBN: 978-1-952869-48-8

Cover Art, Design & Editing by C. M. Tollefson

Cathexis Northwest Press

cathexisnorthwestpress.com

WANTED:

COMEDY, ADDICTS

WANTED:

COMEDY, ADDICTS

WANTED:

COMEDY, ADDICTS

WANTED:

COMEDY, ADDICTS

WANTED:

COMEDY, ADDICTS

WANTED:

COMEDY, ADDICTS

WANTED:

COMEDY, ADDICTS

WANTED:

POEMS BY AR DUGAN

Cathexis Northwest Press

Part I:
I Gather Materials & Ingredients for Thalia

13

Part II:
Almost Parodos

31

Part III:
I Look for Catharsis and Resolution in all the Wrong Places, Find Chimeras Instead

43

Part IV:
Epigraph

53

Part 1:
I Gather Materials & Ingredients for Thalia

Wet paper towels.
The empty cardboard roll.
The Hound's mouth

full of grass. Wadding.
The phone lines
are open.

I'm ready, waiting.
I've dialed, pressed 1 for more.
Said *Go Go Go*. So many times.

Even though touch-tone
and that was
only for rotary.

Me: [breathing]
Phone: "What do you want, little boy?"
Me: [listening]
Phone: "Tell them to leave you alone."

This touch, warm.
This touch, taboo.
I'd say I didn't want to,
but I did.

This touch, red.
I'm not in the same room
at the same bed.
I was never in this room.

The Hound's mouth full of milk.
Paper towels wet still.

Cardboard tube standing by,
per instructions.
Open at both ends.

With the tube
I've made a club.
Turned the insertion point
into the cudgel end
for The Hound's mouth

full of teeth,
Venus flytrap.
The red dot shows
the cordless phone
is still hot.

I hold the phone close
by the proboscis.

The Hound's mouth
full of flies
and fire everywhere.
And water all around
the drying paper towels.

The Hound's mouth:
howl of a dying people
who speak through old books
made from paper towels and milk.

An empty club
holding The Hound's
head up.
Its mouth full of bees.

Soap and water,
they say. Rinse the mouth out.
Foul mouth. The red light
pressed off.

I try another number
I wrote down from the last time
making it red again. The Hound's
clean tongue lolls out
of its white teeth.

How many hours?
The phone whispers: *Taboo*
through canine teeth.
The Hound tells the phone: Go
with its tongue
which has a small
mouth at the tip,
rarely used for talking.

The Hound's tongue's mouth
full of touching
hands (arms and finger nails and
opposable thumbs)
making a new paper towel club
for me.

Inside the paper towel club,
a hollow tunnel
that I fill with skin sauce.

When filled, the club
is a honey canal.
There is a father floating
in a small boat,
hands cupped to his mouth.

In his mouth there are more boats
but with wings
that he throws to me
with the words of his hands.

Part II:
Almost Parodos

I know who you are,
says the father
with his hands.
I'm not your son,
I say to the man
in the boat. *I'm your
brother.*

Let's recap. The brother boats
with buzzing wings are in
The Hound's mouth.
The tongue is a river
with teeth for banks.

The Hound is a natural
predator. A hunter.

To get out of the river
we have to climb over
the teeth into
the mouth itself.

Down the long tube of
The Hound's mouth —
another river
but no boats.

The man who is not the
father says, *this is how
you like it. You could not
stop now — even if you wanted to.*

Someone says, Go
and it echoes in the mouth
cavern like bees with long
snouts that sniff and snuff.

The brother and I
have wasp wings to fly
above the river.
How do we flap them?,
we say.

When I think about moving
my right wing, the brother's
left wing flaps and he
flies in a circle. *I can't
think of both at the same time*,
I yell to him.

Apparently the brother can,
because I am flying straight
down the river,
watching it turn
from red to brown.

The Hound is a natural
pack animal. Think hierarchy.
The Hound is interested
in dominance and submission.
Think alpha. Think omega.

To think the river is filled
with water would be wrong.
It would also be a mistake
to think I saw the brother again.

Part III:
I Look for Catharsis and Resolution in all the Wrong Places, Find Chimeras Instead

I come out the end
of The Hound
with a brother inside
into a pile of wet paper towels.
The red light from the phone
turns everything to smolder.

The phone keeps saying
Call 1-900-... over and over
in a throaty, female cocktail
buzzing a chorus of all the voices
I ever hear on that phone
except the brother's.

I hear a Hound growling
over the din of throaty women
and I know it's time
to make another paper towel club,
but there are none at hand.
The Hound's Mouth,
full of injectables.

The number on the phone's
keypad spells H-O-U-N-D
but when I press ☎
it calls the brother
who now controls
The Hound's mouth.

If I could see
the brother again
I would ask for more
wet paper towels
and cardboard tubes.

But the brother would give me
a phone and a boat to start over.
I call his number on the phone.

He answers as a growling hound
but it sounds just like hound growls
to me. I hit redial — busy signal.

The beeping rhythmic,
like tabula rasa, but it's not.

The phone rings.
On the other end is the sound

of a river rushing. *Hello*, I say.
I'm the brother, I say.

Part IV:
Epigraph

I press ☎ and the fire
ignites below,
inside me,
while its light goes out.

I fill the Hound's mouth
with all the unfinished clubs
and hear myself yelling from inside.
It sounds like muffled buzzing.
Like static. Like a brother
might sound on the phone.

I'd try to talk back
or have the wings
make static noise
but they're back inside
where it's warm
and I have too many
paper things in my mouth.

After swallowing
and before placing
it back in its cradle home,

I kiss and tell
the finally wine-dark phone,
*I'm the brotherHound
and I'm an addict.*

Also Available from Cathexis Northwest Press:

<u>Something To Cry About</u>
by Robert Krantz

<u>Suburban Hermeneutics</u>
by Ian Cappelli

<u>God's Love Is Very Busy</u>
by David Seung

<u>that one time we were almost people</u>
by Christian Czaniecki

<u>Fever Dream/Take Heart</u>
by Valyntina Grenier

<u>The Book of Night & Waking</u>
by Clif Mason

<u>Dead Birds of New Zealand</u>
by Christian Czaniecki

<u>The Weathering of Igneous Rockforms in High-Altitude Riparian Environments</u>
by John Belk

<u>If A Fish</u>
by George Burns

<u>How to Draw a Blank</u>
by Collin Van Son

<u>En Route</u>
by Jesse Wolfe

<u>sky bright psalms</u>
by Temple Cone

<u>Moonbird</u>
by Henry G. Stanton

<u>southern athiest. oh, honey</u>
by d. e. fulford

<u>Bruises, Birthmarks & Other Calamities</u>
by Nadine Klassen

<u>They Curve Like Snakes</u>
by David Alexander McFarland

Cathexis Northwest Press

www.ingramcontent.com/pod-product-compliance
Lightning Source LLC
Chambersburg PA
CBHW012107090526
44592CB00019B/2682